Robots

Stephen White-Thomson

Franklin Watts
First published in Great Britain in 2019 by The Watts Publishing Group
Copyright © The Watts Publishing Group, 2019

Produced for Franklin Watts by
White-Thomson Publishing Ltd
www.wtpub.co.uk

ISBN: 978 1 4451 6483 0 (HB) 978 1 4451 6484 7 (PB)

Credits
Series Editor: Izzi Howell
Book Editor: Stephen White-Thomson
Series Designer: Rocket Design (East Anglia) Ltd
Designer: Clare Nicholas
Literacy Consultant: Kate Ruttle

The publisher would like to thank the following for permission to reproduce their pictures: Alamy: Christian Lademann 4, Josh Gaffen 16, Stocktrek Images, Inc. 19; Getty: Jeff Spicer 7, Tabitha Fireman 9, Andia/UIG 13, The Asahi Shimbun 17, Jeff Spicer 20; Shutterstock: Yullishi cover, BigBlueStudio 5, DeymosHR 6, Ned Snowman 8, Anton Gvozdikov 10, Piotr Wawrzyniuk 12t, tashbulatova 12b, Jenson title page and 14, Zapp2Photo 15, Vadim Sadovski 18, Triff 18, Stocktrek Images, Inc. 19, Andrey Suslov 21, Phonlamai Photo 22.

Every attempt has been made to clear copyright. Should there be any inadvertent omission please apply to the publisher for rectification.

Printed in Dubai

Franklin Watts
An imprint of
Hachette Children's Group
Part of The Watts Publishing Group
Carmelite House
50 Victoria Embankment
London EC4Y 0DZ

An Hachette UK Company
www.hachette.co.uk
www.franklinwatts.co.uk

FSC
MIX
Paper from responsible sources
FSC® C104740

All words in **bold** appear in the glossary on page 23.

Contents

What is a robot?

A robot is a machine controlled by a **computer**. Robots can be **programmed** to do many things that people can do. There are lots of types of robot.

This robot is programmed to sing like a person. ▶

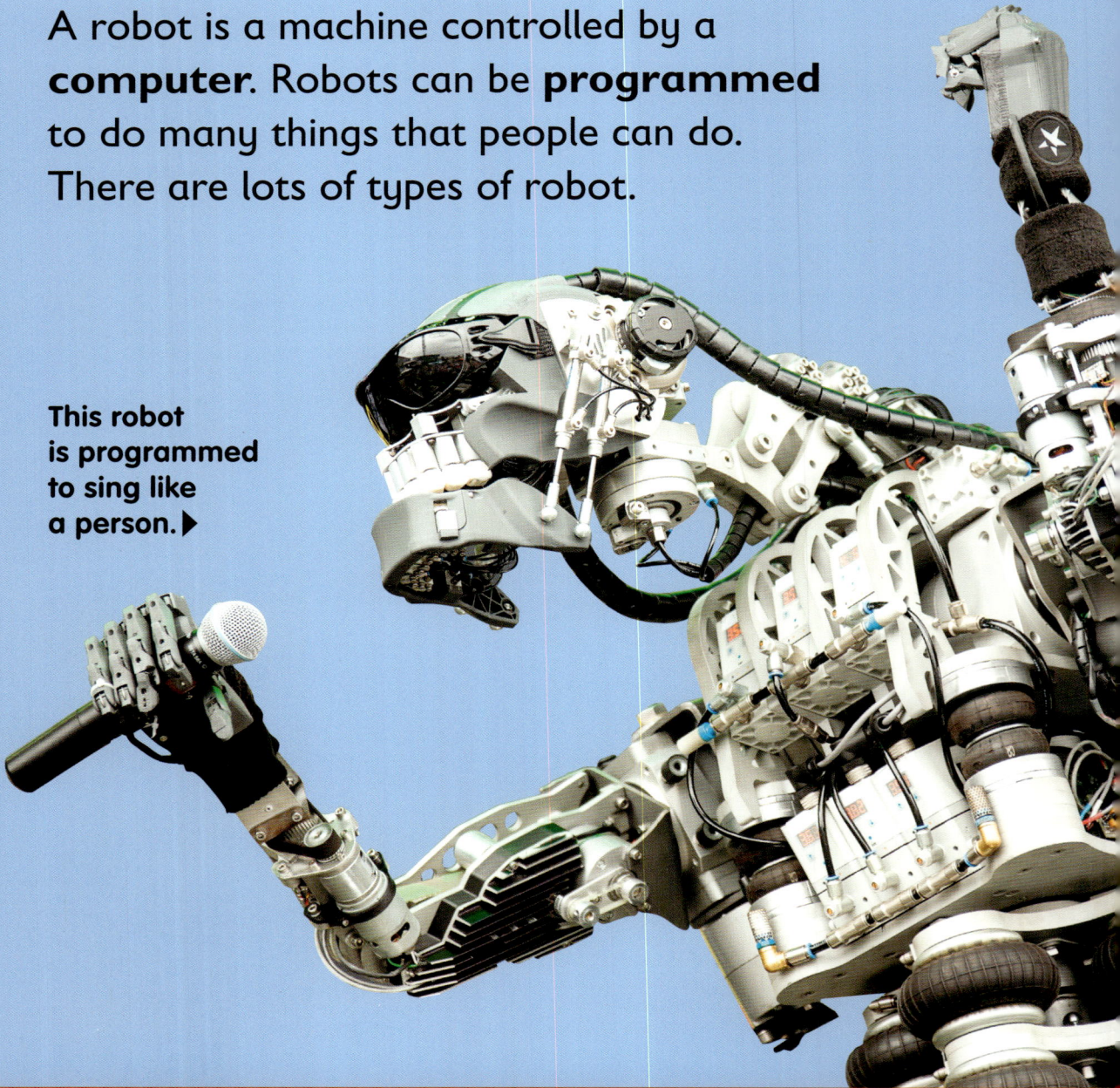

robotic arm

▲ This robotic arm helps people to do difficult work.

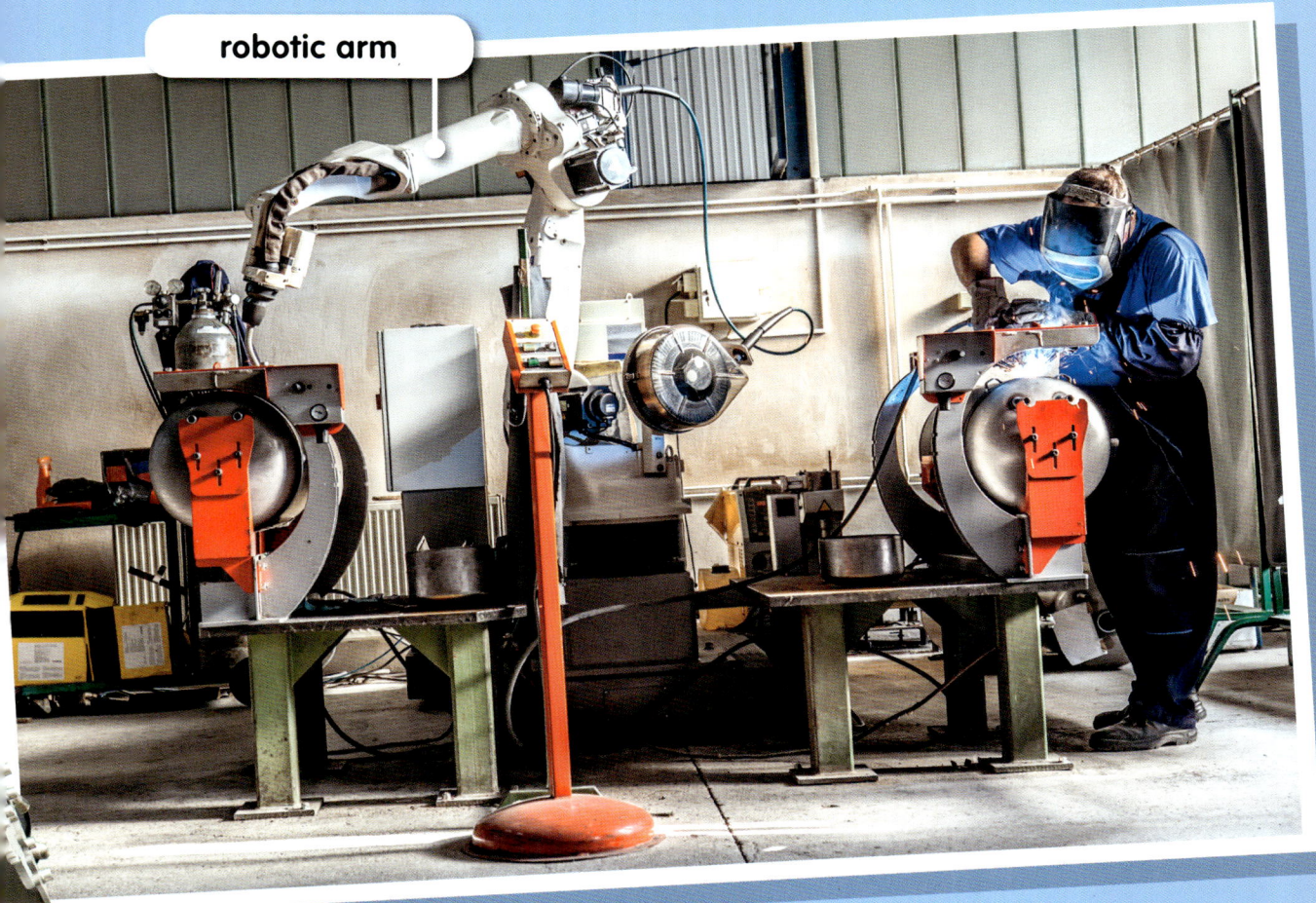

Robots do work that some people don't want to do. They can do things that are dangerous or boring.

Which boring job would you like a robot to help you with?

Humanoid robots

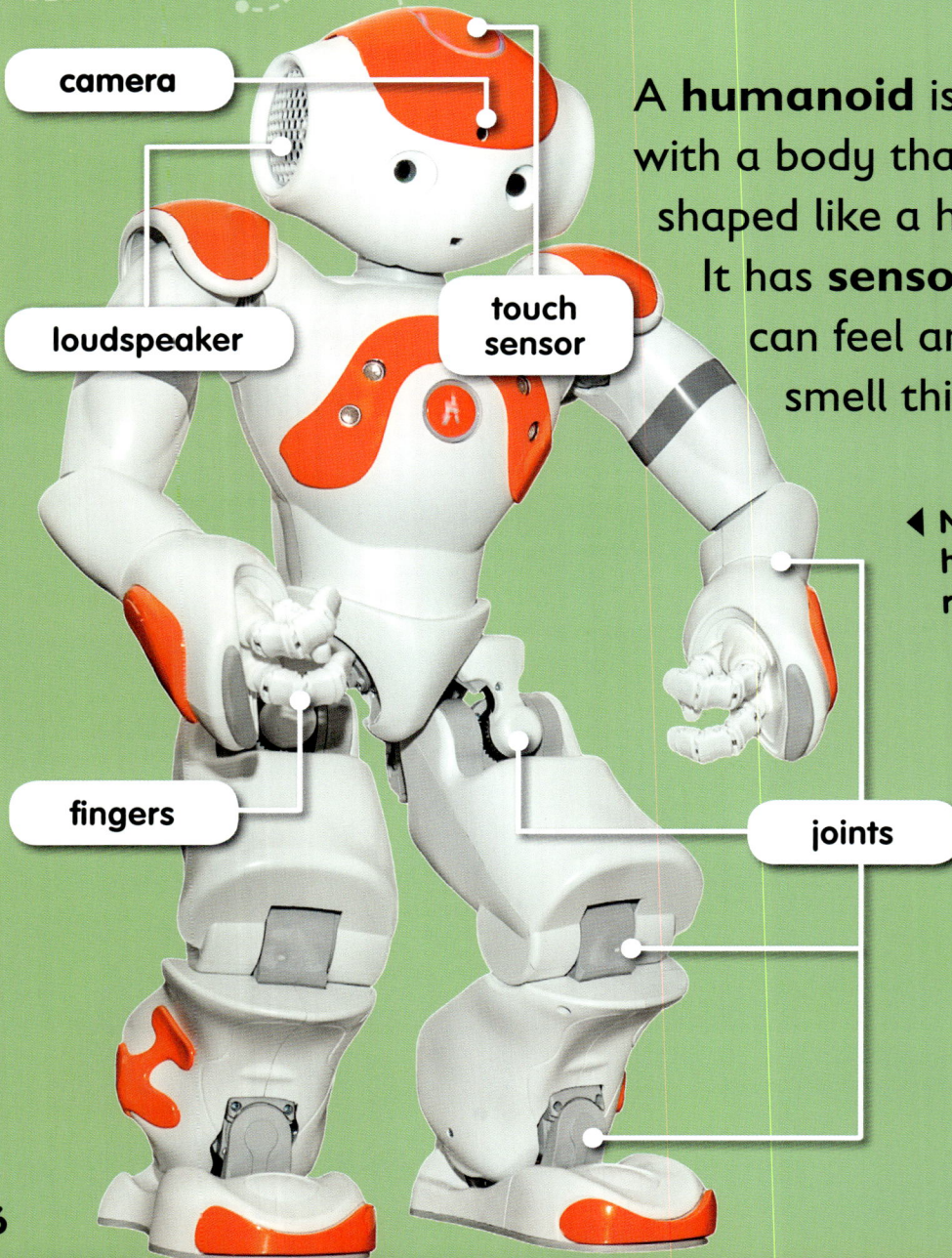

camera

loudspeaker

touch sensor

A **humanoid** is a robot with a body that is shaped like a human. It has **sensors** that can feel and smell things.

◀ Nao is a humanoid robot.

fingers

joints

Robots like Nao have **motors** inside them. If they fall over, they can stand up again. They can even dance!

These children are playing a game with Nao. ▼

What would you ask Nao to do?

Pepper robot

microphone

camera

Pepper is a humanoid robot. It is 1.2 m (4 ft) tall. It listens to what people want to know and tries to help them.

touchscreen tablet

touch sensors

◀ The tablet on Pepper's chest shows you information. Pepper moves on three wheels in its base.

wheels

▼ Pepper tells these children about their train journey – and poses for a selfie!

Pepper robots now work in restaurants and other places. Pepper is programmed to understand your feelings. If you show it you are happy, it will laugh.

Androids

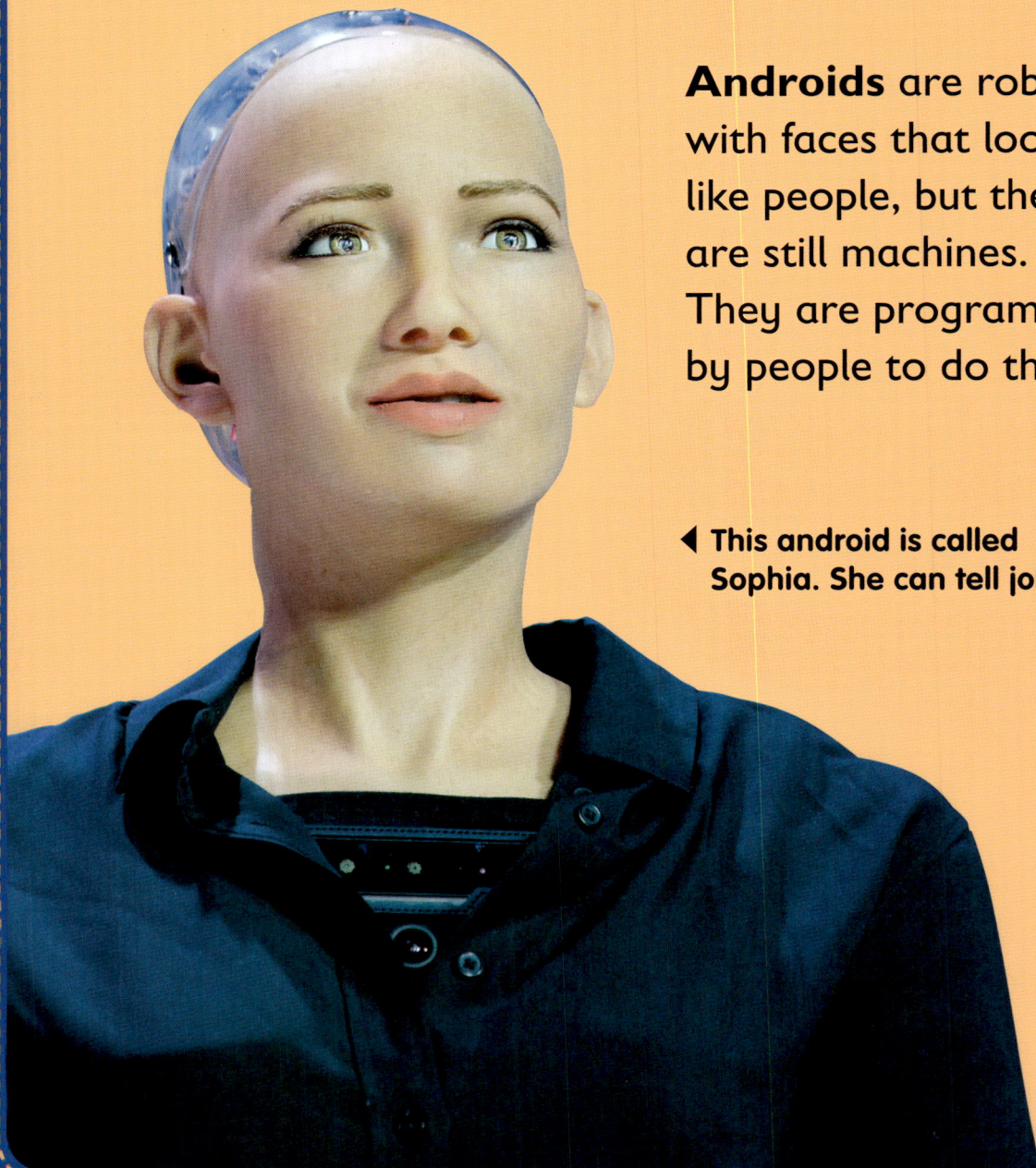

Androids are robots with faces that look like people, but they are still machines. They are programmed by people to do things.

◀ **This android is called Sophia. She can tell jokes!**

Some android robots work in hotels and shopping centres. They can talk and answer questions.

▼ This android gives information to shoppers.

What might shoppers want to know?

Robots at home

Some robots are programmed to help in the home and in the garden.

This robot mows the lawn …

… and this robot vacuums the floor.

Robots that do work around the house are called 'domestic' robots.

What other jobs at home might a robot do?

▲ Soon, robots may be able to cook delicious meals in your home!

Robots at work

Robots can be programmed to do work that is very **precise**. They do some jobs that people used to do.

▼ These robotic arms help put cars together.

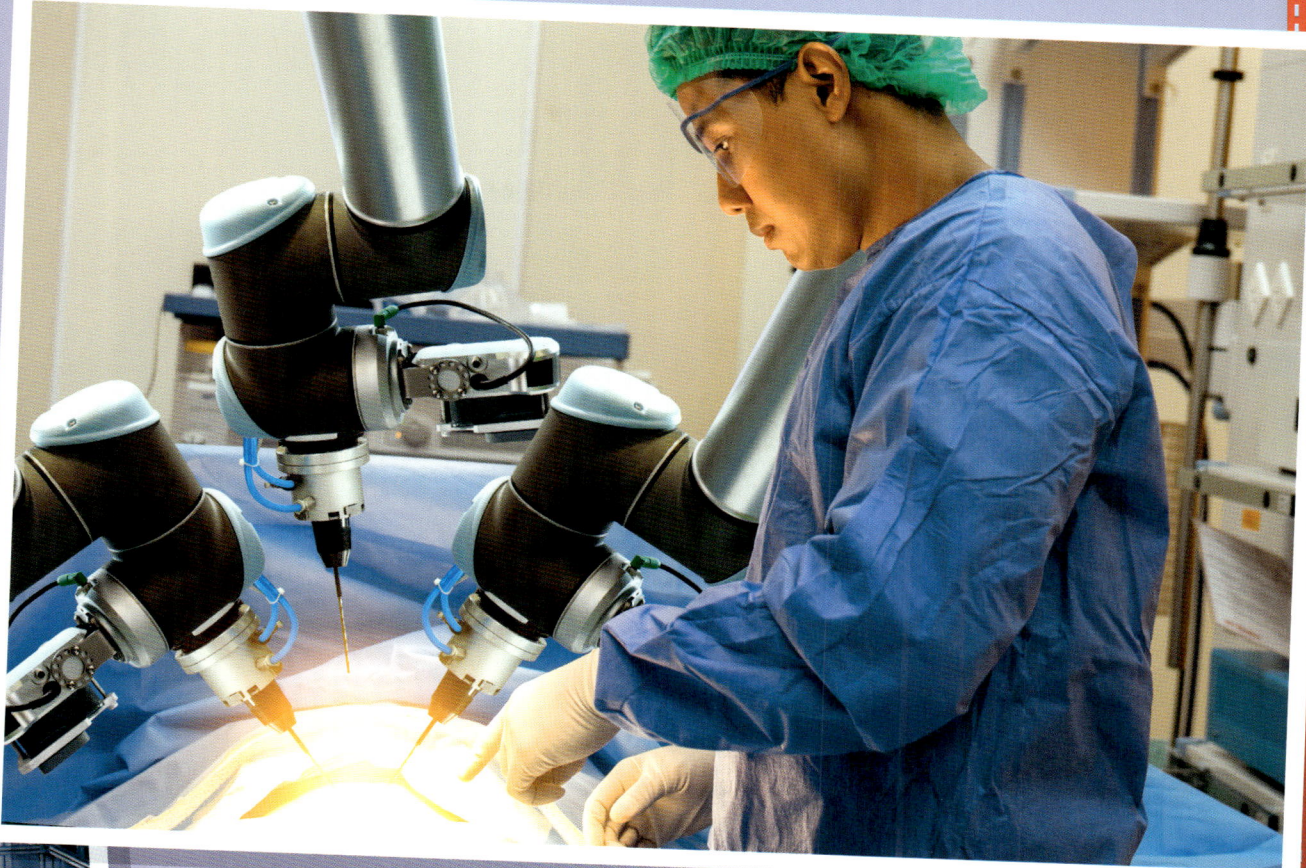

Some robots help **surgeons** to do difficult work. And soon, robots will be able to pick and pack vegetables and fruit.

▲ Robots do not get tired, so they are helpful to surgeons.

Would you be happy to have a robot operate on you?

Toy robots

Miro is a pet toy robot with ears like a rabbit. It can show **emotions**. If Miro is upset, its body will go red. If it is feeling calm, it will go green.

tail

Miro can wag its tail when it is happy! ▶

16

▲ Aibo can even play football!

Aibo is a robot pet. It looks and behaves a bit like a real dog. Aibo can fetch things that you throw for it. It can bark and do tricks for you.

What kind of sensors might Aibo have?

Robots in space

People can't breathe in space. It is a dangerous place, so it is perfect for robots.

Saturn

Cassini

◀ A robot called Cassini explored the **planet Saturn**.

This robot explored the surface of the planet Mars.

Robot **astronauts** help human astronauts to work on the **International Space Station**. They help fix problems inside and outside the Space Station.

▼ Robonaut 2 is a humanoid astronaut that works in space.

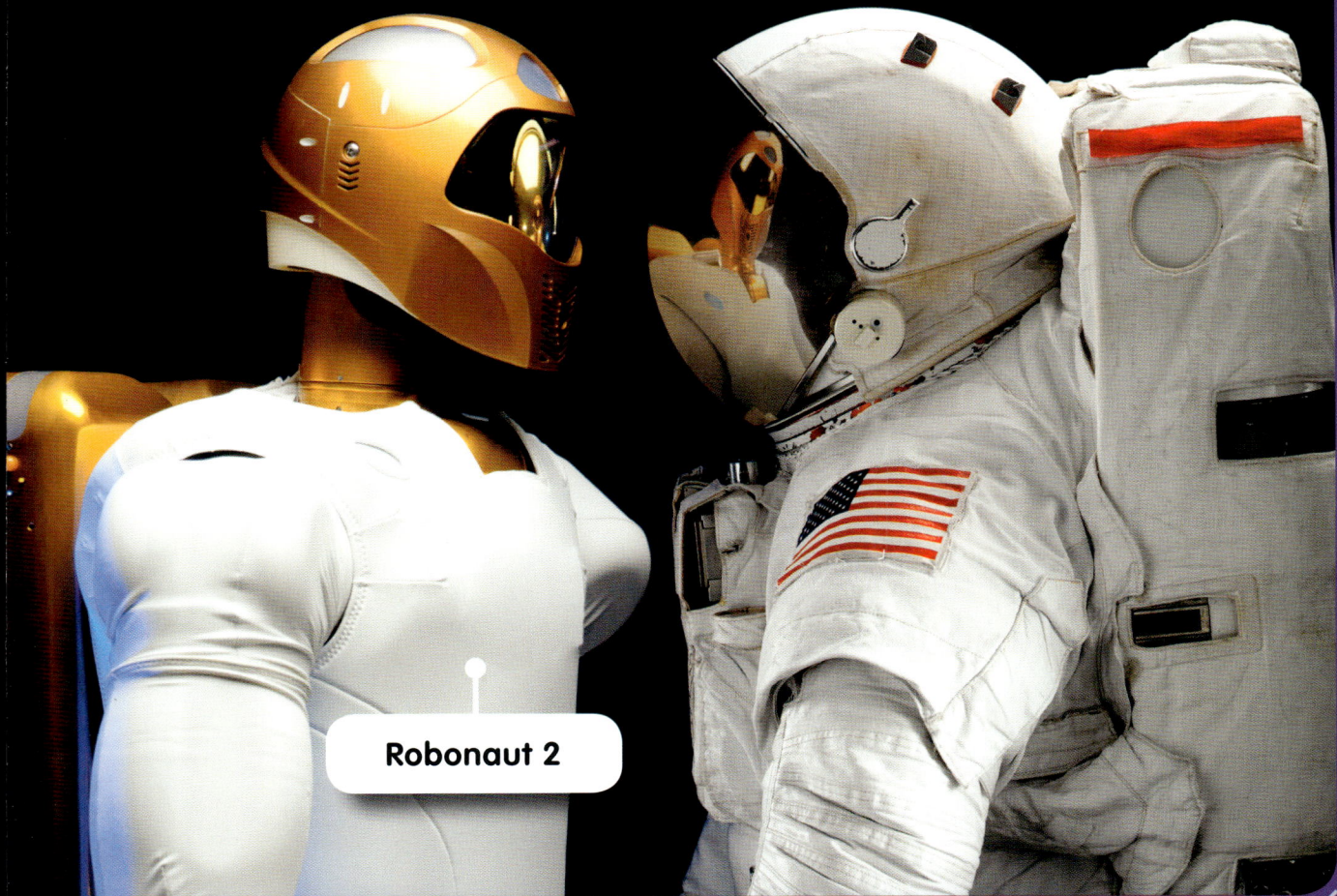

Robonaut 2

The future of robots

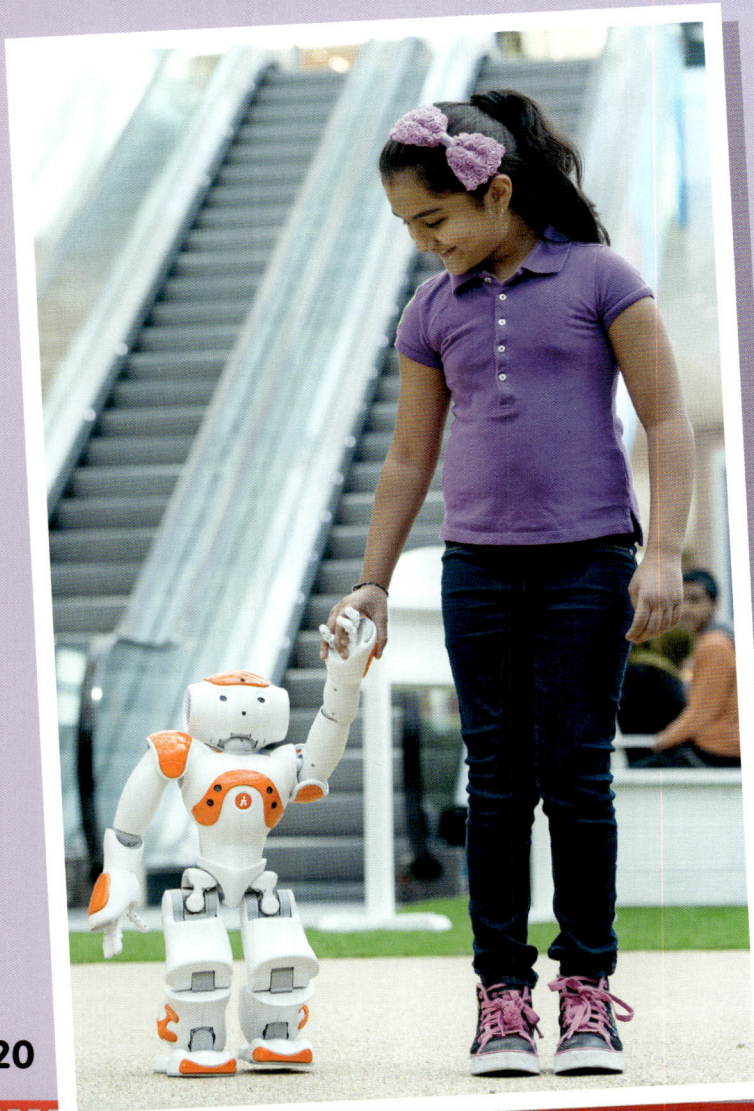

It is hard to know what robots will be able to do for us in the future. But it is likely that they will become part of our everyday lives.

◀ Will robots become our friends?

Robots are becoming cleverer. Some robots are programmed to learn new things for themselves. They will help us more and more in our homes and at work.

Tiny nanorobots may even be able to go inside our bodies and help to keep us healthy! ▼

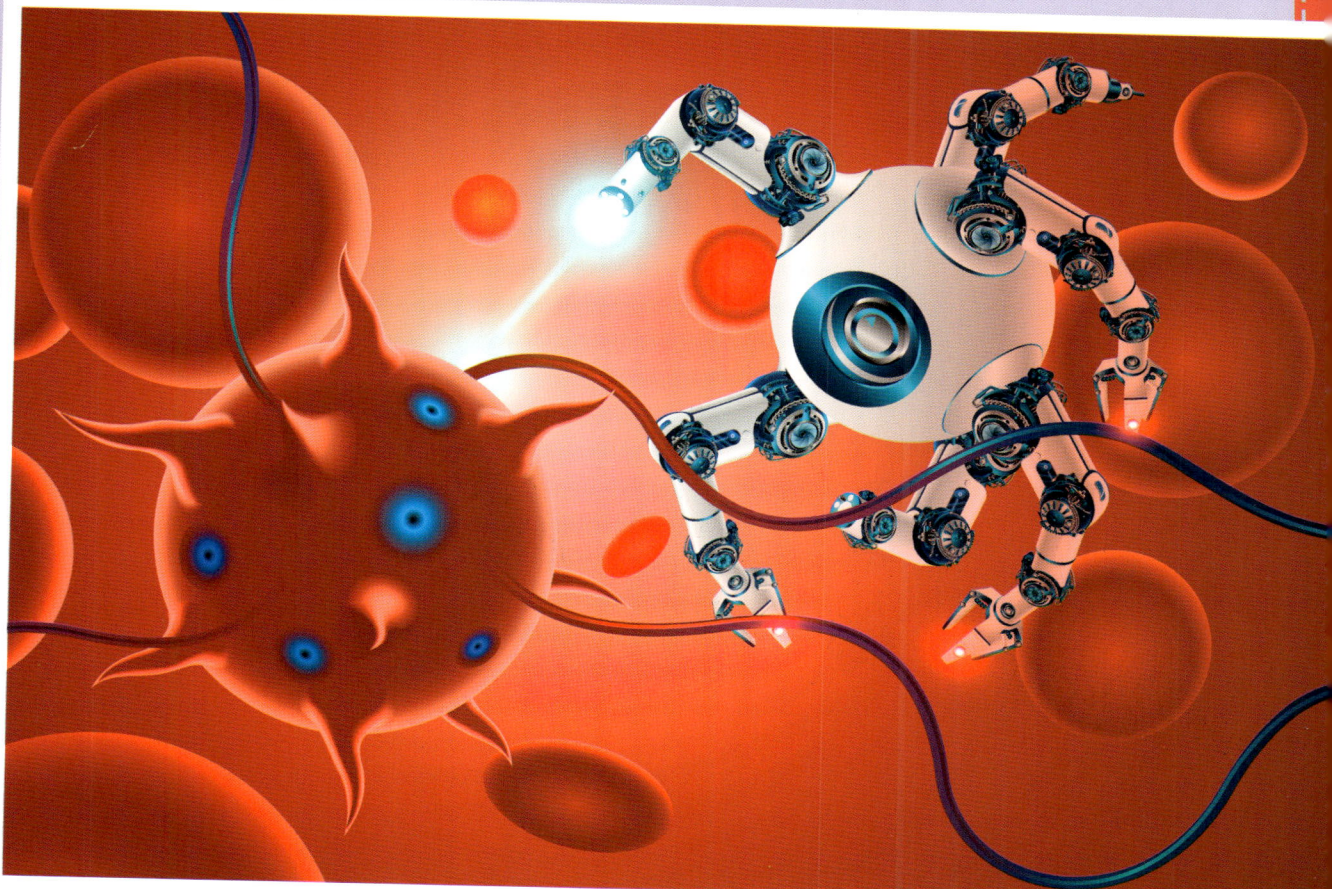

Quiz

Test how much you remember.

Check your answers on page 24.

1 What do you call a robot that has a face like a human?

2 What is the name of a humanoid astronaut?

3 Which robot looks and behaves like a dog?

4 What is the name of robots that work around the house and garden?

5 Name a job a robot does inside the house.

6 What colour does Miro go when it is feeling calm?

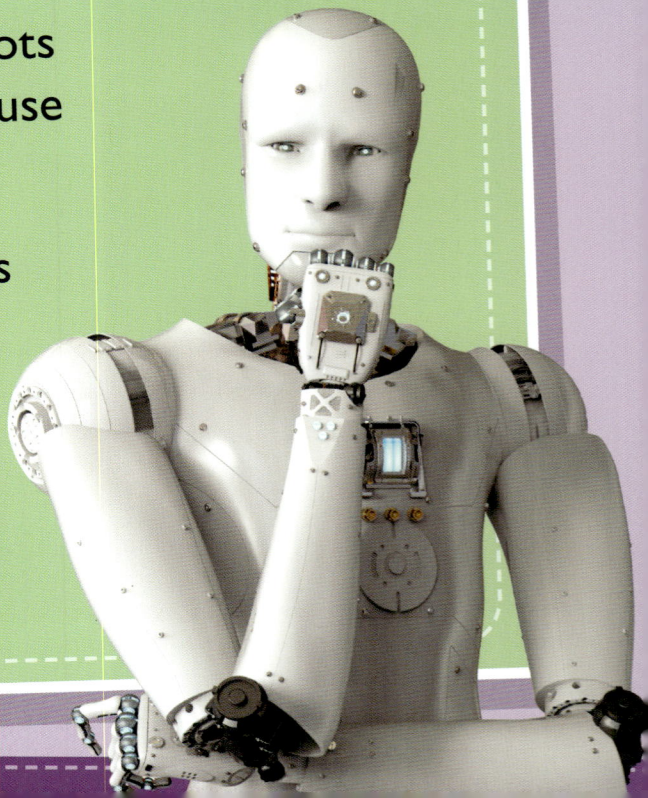

Glossary

android – a robot with a human face

astronaut – someone who travels in space

camera – a machine you use for taking photographs or video

computer – a device for working with information

emotions – strong feelings, such as anger or love

humanoid – a robot with a body that is shaped like a human

International space station – a flying machine in space where astronauts have lived and worked since 2000

microphone – something you speak into when you want to record your voice

motor – an engine that makes something move

nanorobot – a tiny robot too small to see with the human eye

planet – a large round object in space that moves around the Sun or another star

precise – something that is exact and correct

programmed – when you programme a computer, you give it instructions to do something

sensor – a part of a machine, human or animal, that picks up information from around it, such as feeling touch with fingers

surgeon – a doctor who performs operations, often on the inside of bodies

touchscreen tablet – a small computer that you use by touching the screen

Index

Answers:

1: Android; 2: Robonaut 2; 3: Aibo; 4: 'Domestic' robots; 5: Vacuuming the floor; 6: Green

Teaching notes:

Children who are reading Book Band Gold or above should be able to enjoy this book with some independence. Other children will need more support.

Before you share the book:

- What do the children already know about robots? Can they tell you what a robot is?
- Together, list all the robots children have seen in films, cartoons and books and note down what each one can do.

While you share the book:

- Help children to read some of the more unfamiliar words.

- Talk about the questions. Encourage children to think about what they know and what they might want to know about each of the robots.
- Talk about the pictures. Discuss why some robots are humanoid and others aren't.

After you have shared the book

- Talk about why there are different kinds of robots. Reinforce the idea that all robots are built and are programmed to do certain jobs.
- Talk about the people who design, make and programme robots. What kinds of skills and knowledge do they need?
- Work through the free activity sheets at www.hachetteschools.co.uk